WEST SLOPE COMMUNITY LIBRARY
(503)292-6416
MEMBER OF
WASHINGTON COUNTY COOPERATIVE
LIBRARY SERVICES

D0574137

Knight Life

By Jim Gigliotti

PE COMMUNITY LIBRARY
678 SW 78TH AVE
PORTLAND OREGON 97225

Published in the United States of America by The Child's World®
1980 Lookout Drive • Mankato, MN 56003-1705
800-599-READ • www.childsworld.com

ACKNOWLEDGMENTS

The Child's World®: Mary Berendes, Publishing Director

Produced by Shoreline Publishing Group LLC
President / Editorial Director: James Buckley, Jr.
Designer: Tom Carling, carlingdesign.com
Cover: SlimFilms
Assistant Editor: Jim Gigliotti

Photo Credits:
Cover: Dreamstime.com (3)
Interior: AP/Wide World: 26, 29; Dreamstime.com (photographers
listed): Maigi 15, Tatiana Morozova 13, Nicholas rjabow 12,
Vouk27 5; iStock: 11, 16, 17, 18, 19, 21; North Wind Pictures: 9, 10;
Photos.com: 6, 7, 12, 20, 22, 25, 27.

Copyright © 2009 by The Child's World®
All rights reserved. No part of this book may be reproduced or
utilized in any form or by any means without written permission
from the publisher.

LIBRARY OF CONGRESS CATALOG-IN-PUBLICATION DATA

Gigliotti, Jim.
  Knight life / by Jim Gigliotti.
    p. cm. — (Reading rocks!)
  Includes bibliographical references and index.
  ISBN 978-1-60253-100-0 (library bound : alk. paper)
 1. Knights and knighthood—Europe—Juvenile literature. 2.
Civilization, Medieval—Juvenile literature. I. Title. II. Series.

  CR4513.G54 2008
  940.1—dc22

                              2008004481

CONTENTS

THEY WERE LIVING Legends

Brave horsemen . . . exciting adventures . . . men in shining armor riding powerful horses. That's what many people think of when they hear about **medieval** knights.

Stories about knights have been told for hundreds of years—even before they were written down in books. One famous **legend** is that of King Arthur and his Knights of the Round Table. In this legend, King Arthur ruled the kingdom of Camelot. Many knights fought bravely for him.

The king and his knights were said to have held important meetings at a huge, round table.

But knights were more than just stories. They were real people who worked hard at their jobs. For hundreds of years, knights fought in battles, conquered new lands, and protected kings and queens. Knights were very important!

At the round table, all the knights were equals. Everyone had a good seat, and everyone had the same importance.

Artists of long ago often wove portraits or stories on cloth. This weaving shows King Arthur sitting on a throne.

Like most legends, parts of the story aren't true. Arthur probably wasn't a king at all. There were no Knights of the Round Table, either. The real Arthur likely was a military leader in Great Britain. His fame grew as his story was told and retold over hundreds of years.

Arthur didn't even live in the "Age of Knights," which was from about 1066 A.D. to 1500 A.D. Instead, the real Arthur lived hundreds of years before that.

King Arthur may have been a legend, but knights were definitely real. They were real men who were hired as soldiers and protectors. They fought bravely and they acted with honor.

Knights often fought in dangerous battles against other knights.

Imagine that you are living in the late 1400s, and you want to become a knight. Good for you! Like many children of the time, you probably already know how to ride a horse. (All knights must be excellent horse-riders). And let's say that your dad is a knight. That helps—most knights are **descendants** of other knights.

Knights were trained to be very polite and kind to others—especially women.

First, you must leave your home and go to live with a **nobleman**. He will train you in the ways of a knight. At first, you'll be called a **page**. You'll learn

all sorts of important things that a knight has to know, such as good manners and how to dance and play music. Being a knight meant more than fighting in **jousts**, wearing shining armor, and rescuing people!

Knights needed a lot of help to do their jobs. Here you can see a knight (in armor) with his pages.

Pages and squires were trained to help a knight get dressed, whether for battle or for a fancy dance.

After many years of learning proper behavior, it's time for you to go to the next level. When you're about 14, you'll become a **squire**. You'll spend much of your day training for battles and learning how to use weapons. One of a squire's duties is to help a knight get dressed. It's impossible for a knight to put on his armor by himself. A trained squire, though, can do the job quickly.

As a squire, you'll learn the names of the parts of armor. Depending on where you live, there might be 15 or 20 different pieces in an entire suit. It's up to you to keep the pieces clean and ready for battle.

With all your training, you're getting closer to becoming a knight. You're getting closer to the battlefield, too. In fact, you'll have to be there to help if your knight gets knocked off his horse or worse—if he gets injured.

Armor Names

Here are some armor names and the body parts they covered:

gauntlet—hands   gorget—neck
greave—shin   sabaton—foot
pauldron—shoulder   plackart—chest

A king or queen "dubs" a person by tapping a sword on each shoulder.

By the time you're about 21 years old, you can finally become a knight. There is a fancy ceremony headed by a king or queen. He or she taps you on each shoulder with a sword. That's called "dubbing." Once you have been dubbed a knight, other people must call you "Sir." Congratulations, Sir Knight!

Now it's time to go to work. Your new job is at the local castle. Knights are basically workers, or soldiers, looking to be hired. They protect the **lord** and his castle. The knight promises he will be loyal to the lord at all costs—even if that means dying on the battlefield. In return, the lord shelters the knight in his castle. Or perhaps he will provide the knight with his own plot of land.

These actors are re-creating a battle between two knights. Watch out!

KNIGHT
Life

Now that you're a knight, you've got to live like one! First, you need to pick out your colors. Your family already has a **coat of arms**. That's a shield-shaped design with different symbols and colors. Different symbols mean different things. For instance, a lion might mean strength. Coats of arms and their symbols and colors are part of what is called **heraldry** (HAYR-ul-dree).

Before suits of armor, soldiers only had shields to protect themselves. Men decorated their

shields to let people know who owned them. When knights began covering their bodies and faces with armor, heraldry became more important—it let people know who the knight was!

Coats of arms like these identified a knight and his family.

15

As a knight, you'll be living in a castle. But you don't get your own room! Everyone in a castle ate, worked, and slept in the same big rooms. In later years, the lords or kings and queens began making their own rooms in their castles.

Castles were made of thick, heavy stones. A flag would tell visitors who owned the castle.

But everyone else still had to share.

Castles could get very cold in the winter and very hot in the summer. But they were luxurious compared to the shelters of the peasants who lived outside the castle walls. Castles showed off a king's wealth and power. Richer kings could build huge, fancy castles that had lots of ways to keep invaders out. Poorer kings or lords had smaller, simpler castles.

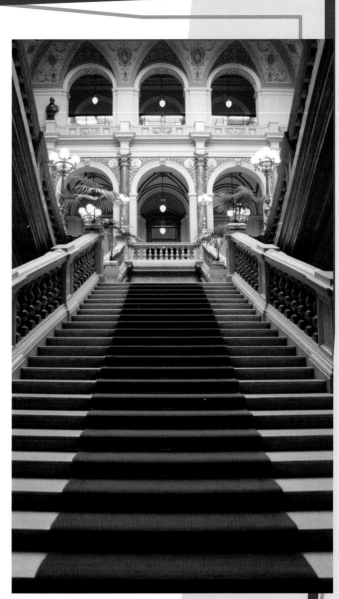

Fancy castles sometimes had huge staircases.

Even though you have a job, you must still practice, practice, practice. If you're lucky, nobody will try to invade your king's land or take over his castle. But just in case, you have to keep your fighting skills in top shape.

Your fighting skills are the ones you'll use in battle. These skills include riding a horse in battle and

Knight Weapons

The sword was a knight's main weapon. But knights also used daggers, battle-axes, lances, and maces. A mace was a club with a heavy, spiked ball. This picture shows a weapon called a flail—it's a mace with a chain.

learning how to swing a sword the right way!

You might also use other weapons such as lances, axes, or clubs. Knowing how to move well in heavy armor might save your life in a battle one day.

Knights needed to know how to fight both on the ground and on horseback.

All your practice will come in handy at a **tournament**. Early tournaments, or competitions among knights, used real weapons. Some knights were injured or even killed.

Kings and lords soon realized that the tournaments should be safer. They wanted their knights and horses healthy for the real battles. Rules were made, and tournaments began using points to track the winners. Weapons were rounded off so fewer knights got hurt.

Jousting became very popular in the 1300s. It was a dangerous and sometimes deadly sport.

The barrier
between the
two jousters
prevented the
horses from
colliding with
each other.

The joust became the tournament's big event. In a joust, knights would ride toward each other on horseback. They would jab with a long lance and try to knock the other knight off his horse.

Tournaments became big social events. A knight could earn a great **reputation**—and maybe a better job—if he won a tournament.

Knights had to believe in God and follow the rules of the church.

Medieval knights were taught
to be courageous, honest, loyal,
trustworthy, courteous, and humble.
They learned how to treat others—
even their enemies—in a noble way.
If prisoners were captured during a
battle, knights were taught to treat
them with respect. Knights also
learned how to behave if they were
ever captured themselves.

Most importantly, knights had a
way of behaving called **chivalry**
(SHIV-uhl-ree). Chivalry taught
knights to be respectful and polite
at all times—especially to women.
Chivalry also meant having very
good manners, particularly when
courting. Being a knight meant not
only fighting well, but acting right!

This is the old-time word for "dating." Knights had to follow many rules when courting women.

SHINING
Armor

Now, let's get you ready for battle. You'll need to wear full armor, although the earliest knights didn't wear the famous "shining armor." The first knights wore simple armor that was called "chain mail," or just "mail." Mail was made from small, linked iron rings. Put together enough of these rings, and you had an outfit that could protect a knight.

The trouble was, it took thousands and thousands of links to make a piece of armor that was big enough to cover a knight. Chain mail was heavy and uncomfortable. Not only that—it didn't offer much protection! An enemy's sword could still pierce through the spaces in the rings.

Later knights learned that small pieces of chain mail worn around the chest area—but under the armor—offered the best protection.

Tightly packed links of metal like these form chain mail.

OPPOSITE PAGE
A knight wearing a full suit of armor was well protected.

In movies, you might see knights wearing clunky, clumsy suits of armor. Real warriors couldn't fight in suits like these. Instead, pieces of steel were molded for various parts of a knight's body. The pieces had hinges to make it easier for a knight to move around.

Modern "Knights"

Wearing a full suit of armor meant a knight was carrying an extra 50 pounds (23 kg) of weight. He had to be in really good shape! That's nothing compared to today's soldiers, however. A soldier in the U.S. Army carries nearly 80 pounds (36 kg) of supplies and weapons while in combat.

The biggest problem with wearing a suit of armor was the heat. It got really hot in there! Even so, suits offered much better protection than chain mail. A shot from an arrow that might break through chain mail couldn't penetrate armor. A thrust from a sword would just slide off the curved plate of steel.

A knight no longer needed a shield, either. After all, he was covered from head to toe in steel! Now he was ready to go to battle.

A suit of armor made a knight a powerful opponent. So did his many years of training for the job. By about 1500 A.D., however, the Age of Knights was ending. One reason was that governments were building large armies. Smaller bands of knights weren't needed.

When guns (like this one carried by a Spanish soldier) were introduced, the Age of Knights came to an end.

The biggest reason for the end of the Age of Knights was the invention of the gun. Guns were better weapons, and regular people could use them. A person didn't have to have years of training to use a gun (as knights did for swordfighting). The Age of Knights was over.

Good Knights

There may not be any more knights in shining armor, but that doesn't mean there aren't any more knights. The Queen of England still dubs knights—but today they're British citizens who have made special contributions to society (such as Sir Paul McCartney, shown here). Even some Americans, like Bill Gates, have been made honorary knights.

Even though it has been hundreds of years since the age of medieval knights, people are still fascinated by them. Actors still dress up in suits of armor and hold jousts for you to see. And we can look to knights as examples of how to act with honesty, courage, and chivalry. You can be a modern-day knight— without all the fighting!

GLOSSARY

chivalry behaving in a very polite way, especially to girls or women

coat of arms a shield-shaped design with different symbols and colors

courting dating

descendants a later generation; you are a descendant of your parents and grandparents

heraldry the study of coats of arms

joust a battle on horseback in which two people ride toward each other and try to knock the other person off his or her horse

legend a story (one that has been told for many years) that hasn't been proven to be true

lord a man who ruled over a large area of land (and people) during the Middle Ages

medieval having to do with the Middle Ages, a time in history from about 500 A.D. to 1450 A.D.

nobleman a respected person of high rank in society

page a boy servant between the ages of 7 and 14

reputation how a person is thought of by other people

squire a servant, training to be a knight, who was between the ages of 14 and 21

tournament in the Middle Ages, a tournament was a competition among knights; the joust was a tournament's big event

FIND OUT MORE

BOOKS

Knight (DK Eyewitness Books)
By Christopher Gravett (DK, 2007)
Filled with hundreds of pictures, this book traces the history of knights and includes information about their lives on and off the battlefields.

Knights and Castles
By Mary Pope and Will Osborne
(Random House Books for Young Readers, 2000)
The authors of the fictional Magic Tree House series give you a look at their research notebooks for the many tales they've set in medieval times.

The Medieval World
By Philip Steele (Kingfisher Books, 2006)
This book takes you into medieval life, whether in a castle, a village, or in the countryside. Meet the people the knights were protecting!

WEB SITES

Visit our Web site for lots of links about knights and their lives and times: www.childsworld.com/links

Note to Parents, Teachers, and Librarians: We routinely check our Web links to make sure they're safe, active sites—so encourage your readers to check them out!

INDEX

JIM GIGLIOTTI is a freelance writer who lives in southern California with his wife and two children. A former editor at the National Football League, he has written more than two dozen books for youngsters.

11-09 J
940.1
GIG